YOUR KNOWLEDGE HAS VALUE

AF144748

- We will publish your bachelor's and master's thesis, essays and papers

- Your own eBook and book - sold worldwide in all relevant shops

- Earn money with each sale

Upload your text at www.GRIN.com and publish for free

Bibliographic information published by the German National Library:

The German National Library lists this publication in the National Bibliography; detailed bibliographic data are available on the Internet at http://dnb.dnb.de .

Imprint:

Copyright © 2019 GRIN Verlag
Print and binding: Books on Demand GmbH, Norderstedt Germany
ISBN: 9783346037060

This book at GRIN:

https://www.grin.com/document/502571

Charles Okeke

The prospects of African youth in the labour market across the border between Africa and China

GRIN Verlag

GRIN - Your knowledge has value

Since its foundation in 1998, GRIN has specialized in publishing academic texts by students, college teachers and other academics as e-book and printed book. The website www.grin.com is an ideal platform for presenting term papers, final papers, scientific essays, dissertations and specialist books.

Visit us on the internet:

http://www.grin.com/

http://www.facebook.com/grincom

http://www.twitter.com/grin_com

THE PROSPECTS OF AFRICAN YOUTH IN THE LABOUR MARKET ACROSS THE BORDER BETWEEN AFRICA AND CHINA

Charles Okeke

PhD (International Law) Candidate

University of International Business & Economics (UIBE), Beijing

Abstract

This paper seeks to explore the conundrum of the African youth in the labour market as the number of young people continues to grow with a few job openings available for them. There is no unique determinant of the youth employment challenge in the African region. Rather, a combination of factors contributes to compound a situation that has become a top socio-political priority for the region.

Africa has the youngest population in the world and over 10 years from now, 30 million young people from the region are likely to enter the African labour market each year.[1]

The African population is very young and therefore, one could say that the employment challenge is, in effect, also a youth challenge. Young people are between 1.5 and 2.5 times more likely to be out of work than older adults in most of the countries in the continent.

Africa's unemployment conundrum is such that those in vulnerable employment and those underemployed in informal sectors are not always in the calculation when assessing the dangers of lack of jobs for young people.[2] Youth find work but most often than not, in places where the pay is very low with lack of opportunity for skills development and job security.

This is so, partly because most African countries have not been able to transform fundamentally from low productivity agriculture to higher productivity on-agriculture sectors and when coupled with high fertility and low infant mortality, the result has shown little improvement in the building of sustainable employment structure.

---

[1] "Youth Employment in Africa (Africa)." Youth Employment in Africa (Africa), www.ilo.org/africa/areas-of-work/youth-employment/lang--en/index.htm.

[2] "Africa's Jobless Youth Cast a Shadow over Economic Growth | Africa Renewal." United Nations, United Nations, www.un.org/africarenewal/magazine/special-edition-youth-2017/africas-jobless-youth-cast-shadow-over-economic-growth.

Over the past few years, researches have been carried out on several dimensions of China's education, training and labour relations with Africa. In spite of China's discourse about the parity and importance of win-win in China–Africa engagement, many still think that China has not paid sufficient attention to the issue of job creation for the young people in Africa, considering the number of investments the country has in the continent.

Many Chinese companies operating in Africa have a negative assessment card. Beyond the claim of asymmetric relations and debt-trap diplomacy, when it comes to their employment record, some observers accuse the Chinese of mainly employing their citizens for projects in Africa, depriving the locals of potential jobs. When they do hire locally, the accusation is that the wages are very low and come with little or no training. But this view has come largely from the West who hitherto has not seen anything good in the Sino-Africa relations.[3]

Keywords: Africa, China, Employment, Government, Labour, Opportunities, Unemployment, Youth

1. Introduction

The word youth has no universally accepted definition. The understanding, however, is that youth depends on ages, social positions, and functions they carry out in a place, era, etc. The time of youth could be agreed to be between childhood and adulthood; it is a transition period with non-definite boundaries.[4] The transition from youth to adulthood is usually within the ambit of issues such as physiological, psychological, social, and financial freedom. There are numerous ways to attaining adult status, and we can see the possibility of an increase in the transition ages. To that effect, youth represent a very heterogeneous group.[5]

Presently, Africa is the continent with the youngest population in the world. It is believed that one of five persons in the region falls within 15 and 24. As of 2010, the age group of youths in Africa reached 205 million and could reach nearly 437 million by 2050, or 33.3% of all people age 15–24 in the world.[6]

---

[3] "Africa: Study Reveals Chinese Companies Pay & Train Workers to Similar Standards as Non-Chinese Companies." Business & Human Rights Resource Centre, 17 July 2019, www.business-humanrights.org/en/africa-study-reveals-chinese-companies-pay-train-workers-to-similar-standards-as-non-chinese-companies.
[4] "Emerging Adulthood." Noba, nobaproject.com/modules/emerging-adulthood.
[5] ibid
[6] Développement, Agence Française de, and Objectif-Developpement. "Supporting Youth Insertion into the African Labor Market." Issuu, issuu.com/objectif-developpement/docs/youth_insertion_web.

In spite of the increasing number of rural-urban migration, close to 70% of Africans still live in rural areas.[7] The problems young people encounter in becoming a part of the work-force and develop the required skills to ensure gainful and productive employment is crucial in the development and prospects for the growth of any society.

Africa, particularly South-Sahara Africa has the youngest region people in the world, and this is expected to continue in the foreseeable future. The average age is 18 now, which is 7 years younger than South Asia, with the second youngest population in the world and expectedly will rise to 24 by 2050.

Africa's youth category is large and growing rapidly. Between 2000 and 2015, the 15 and 24 age group grew by 2.6% each year on average. According to UN estimates, there were 190 million in this age group as of 2015, and this number is expected to increase at an annual rate of 2.5–2.7%, reaching 249 million in 2025, and 311 million in 2035.[8]

2. Why is youth unemployment an important topic for Africa?

Unemployment for young people is a global epidemic and Africa cannot be isolated when we discuss the problems that are associated with it. However, the case of Africa is our focus in this paper, importantly, because the number of youth in the region is on the rise and that might spell doom if the labour market does not have what it takes to accommodate this number.

African countries are diverse but they have some tendencies in common, and one of them is a strong demographic growth; a large number of young people in the continent are continuously seeking for an improved welfare and financial independence which the labour market is expected to provide, to a large extent, this dream is far from realized.[9]

Young people in Africa, both in the urban and rural concentrations need jobs, the potential is there but the opportunities are mostly lacking. The limited education system also has impaired the expansion of the labour market, leaving a lot of young school leavers in little or no demand.

---

[7] Betcherman, Gordon, and Themrise Khan. "Jobs for Africa's Expanding Youth Cohort: a Stocktaking of Employment Prospects and Policy Interventions." SpringerLink, Springer Berlin Heidelberg, 12 July 2018, link.springer.com/article/10.1186/s40176-018-0121-y.

[8] Betcherman, Gordon, and Themrise Khan. "Jobs for Africa's Expanding Youth Cohort: a Stocktaking of Employment Prospects and Policy Interventions." SpringerLink, Springer Berlin Heidelberg, 12 July 2018, link.springer.com/article/10.1186/s40176-018-0121-y.

[9] "Facing the Growing Unemployment Challenges in Africa." Facing the Growing Unemployment Challenges in Africa, 20 Jan. 2016, www.ilo.org/africa/media-centre/pr/WCMS_444474/lang--en/index.htm.

While the continent looks up to the youth for growth, the social and professional fitting is presently unstable amidst an increasing level of poverty.[10]

This debacle presents real issues for politicians, who first of all, need to tame urban-rural migration while cautiously managing the possible fallout of social and political unrest that might ensue when the youth get fed-up with their plight. We have seen that in some countries in the region with the rise of crimes such as kidnapping and terrorism among others.

3. Youth employment trends

In the book, "The Industrial Experience of Tanzania" edited by Szirmai et al it posited that the empirical analysis of employment in sub-Saharan Africa is only derived from household surveys, such as labor force surveys and living standards measurement surveys. In many countries of Africa, regular surveys are not conducted except for Tanzania, South Africa, and Mauritius. The others don't have national coverage to ascertain the employment rate.

Recently, efforts from international organizations such as the World Bank, International Labour Organization, and African Economic Outlook, etc. to harmonize existing household surveys have been relied upon when discussing the subject of youth employment among the various countries of the continent.

Youth employment in Africa, however, holds its own when compared to other regions around the world. The unemployment rate among young population is below the rate in many places except for South and East Asia and the ratio between the youth and adult unemployment rates is the lowest among all regions.[11] A higher percentage of young people in the continent participate in the labor force and employed more than what can be obtained in other regions.

4. Obstacles to better jobs for African youth

The big issues facing Africa today are not youth-related. Lack of infrastructure, good leadership, lack of proper accountability, access to credit among many others; [12] but the irony is that these problems somehow affect the level of job opportunities in a country because a low level of development means a low level of jobs in the market. For instance, in lower-income economies

---

[10] "Africa's Jobless Youth Cast a Shadow over Economic Growth | Africa Renewal." United Nations, United Nations, www.un.org/africarenewal/magazine/special-edition-youth-2017/africas-jobless-youth-cast-shadow-over-economic-growth.
[11] idrc.ca/sites/default/files/sp/Documents%20EN/Youth_Employment_Sub-Saharan_Africa_WEB_FINAL.pdf
[12] "Youth Employment in Sub-Saharan Africa." World Bank, www.worldbank.org/en/programs/africa-regional-studies/publication/youth-employment-in-sub-saharan-africa.

where the people depend largely on agriculture, low productivity would be a major constraint to a good livelihood.

Employers and enterprises in Africa are often reluctant about hiring young people, blaming it on lack of experience, expertise, and personal immaturity. At the same time, they make no effort to put money and time into training young people, preferring to hire more experienced adult workers.

An improved result in youth engagement in the labour market will require an effort on the demand side if there is going to be a flourishing economic environment, be it in agriculture or micro-businesses, or even in the wage sector of the economy. These could be seen as general problems, but these demand impediments can boomerang and the youth will be the ones to pay the ultimate price. For example, credit may be difficult to get in many African countries, but the fact remains that the chances for young business people to access it are remote;[13] furthermore, lack of well-equipped schools, job opportunities by the government and private sector and improved labour laws should be looked into and corrected.

5. Youth in Africa and employment opportunities created by Sino-Africa Relations

Of the over 10,000 Chinese companies operating in Africa, only a few rely on the locals, most of the others recruit minimal local labour, they instead rely tremendously on Chinese migrant labour in their infrastructure and public construction jobs. This school of thought has been countered by some academics who argue that there are no empirical figures to back the claim, stressing that it is not easy to get the exact numbers of African workers in Chinese companies due to the lack of official statistics.

The Ministry of Finance of Angola published a report, which featured the make-up of employees in 30 infrastructure projects completed by Chinese companies around the country. In a total of 3136 workers, 1872 were Angolans, making up 59.7 percent of the entire work-force. Buttressing the argument that the number of Chinese workers is still relatively high since it is over 40 percent.[14]

Reports on the construction of the Chinese-funded Imboulou dam in Congo Brazzaville witnessed as many as 2,000 locals, 400 Chinese and 20 German workers. Employment statistics in five operating Chinese economic zones reiterated the numbers in line with records from other quarters.[15]

---

[13] ibid
[14] Adams AV, Johansson de Silva S, Razmara S. Improving skills development in the informal sector: strategies for sub-Saharan Africa. Washington, DC: World Bank; 2013.
[15] "China-Africa Ties Should Create Jobs for the Youth." Www.sidint.net, www.sidint.net/content/china-africa-ties-should-create-jobs-youth.

There is no gainsaying that China has become the partner of choice of many African countries. More and more Chinese firms are trooping into the region and the reception has been very warm just like in the past.

The main areas of Chinese investments in Africa are in infrastructure, agriculture, mining, finance, transportation, and trade. Many African leaders say the presence of China in the region is a good thing considering that most investments are carried out with no political strings like those coming from countries in the West. As Africa is reported to be the fastest-growing economy in the world, China has played a significant role in making that reality of our time.

As Africa is hailed as rising, there is still plenty to worry about and most disturbing is youth unemployment and underemployment which keeps rising in many countries in the region. Currently, it is reported that 70 percent of unemployed people in Africa are young people.

Commentators believe that China can play a big role in bolstering the labour market in Africa. Chinese companies are encouraged to invest more in the youth by allowing them to do the jobs that many Chinese are brought in as expats to do; all it takes is to develop their technical skills and prepare them for the work ahead.

Recently, China signed a deal with the government of Kenya which has been lauded as progressive as it targets the young population in the country. The Kenyan National Youth Service popularly dubbed the NYS was created in 1964 shortly after independence when education opportunities were largely limited.

The support from China has raised some bit of hope among the youth in Kenya as the NYS is about to be resuscitated and put back to the state it was many years when it was conceived. Observers are excited and hopeful that the revived NYS will help tackle the problem of rising youth unemployment in the country.

In the area of manufacturing, China was ahead of many countries for so many years; however, things are beginning to change as the country begins to witness the rise of industrial labour cost. Presently, most factories see this rise in cost as the main impediment for continuous production.[16]

This latest development could offer great opportunity for a region like Africa which can provide relatively lower labour cost and abundance of raw minerals for production. Some analysts have predicted that if just 1 percent of China's production of garments is moved to Africa, the continent production and export of garments would be bolstered by at least 47 percent

---

[16] Cleland, J. (2017). Population growth, employment, and livelihoods: the triple challenge. Journal of Demographic Economics, 83(01), 51–61

One of the countries that have benefitted from this situation is Ethiopia; the East African country has started an ambitious industrial park development project to provide the infrastructure and incentives for investors in light manufacturing industries.

At the moment, four parks are already operational, with many others still under construction. The country expects to maximize every opportunity that comes with China's "going out" policy by building at least 30 industrial parks by 2020.[17] Official government reports say about 28,000 jobs have been created for the young people since the inception of the first park.

In 2018, the Chinese leader, Xi Jinping stressed that future Sino-African cooperation should focus on the youth. He used the occasion of the Forum on China and Africa Cooperation (FOCAC) to emphasize on the importance of the alliance to develop young people in Africa.

In the first quarter of 2018 for example, the unemployment rate among South Africans aged 15–34 was 38.2%. In the same age group across the rest of the continent, nearly a third is unemployed, according to an African Development Bank report. This situation, which can be seen in many other countries within the continent prompted China to make the promise of working with African leaders in training and empowering young people.

6. How African youth can further capture jobs created by China

The World Economic Forum's Human Capital Index report themes: The Future of Jobs and Skills in Africa, Preparing the Region for the Fourth Industrial Revolution, which was made public in 2017 reported that sub-Saharan Africa currently uses 55 percent of its human capital potential, compared with a global average of 65 percent.[18]

The report further stated that most employers across the continent identify lack of skilled workforce as a big drawback on the growth of their businesses, the report carried out its survey in Tanzania with 41 percent of all companies in that country reporting the trend, 30 percent in Kenya, 9 percent in South Africa and 6 percent in Nigeria.[19]

This pattern needs to change if the youth are to grab the opportunities that will come with more Chinese investments in the region and trade. Capacity building is paramount to bridge that gap which has impeded the success of industrialization in Africa. Governments need to concentrate more on capacity building and as it would be the panacea to good economic performance in the short and long run.

[17] Tilman Altenburg Head, Transformation of Economic and Social Systems Programme, German Development Institute / Deutsches Institut für Entwicklungspolitik (DIE)
[18] 胡雨濛   . "JOBS   FOR   AFRICA."   JOBS   FOR   AFRICA   -   World   -   Chinadaily.com.cn, www.chinadaily.com.cn/a/201803/31/WS5abe80aba3105cdcf6515763.html.
[19] ibid

African governments have been alerted by pundits that they are running out of time if they fail to capture the abundant jobs outsourced by China in recent times in the wake of the fifth industrial revolution.

According to the World Bank projection, the rising wages in China, as well as the government's commitment to upgrade its manufacturing industries, will see the country release around 83 million to 85 million jobs, providing unequaled industrialization opportunities for low-income economies, particularly for Africa.

7. Conclusion

Africa needs to work more closely with their Chinese counterparts to create more job programmes. They could start by creating short-term job opportunities, including community services programme for unskilled youth, and a graduate internship scheme, which will help university graduates to acquire work experience in private-sector businesses.

Africa's development is under danger if the issue of youth unemployment is not critically addressed. The continent cannot afford to exclude young people from economic opportunities that will encourage them to propel to the next orbit and contribute to the economic growth of their countries.

Politicians in Africa should approach the youth unemployment dilemma in two crucial ways; which is by helping to improve the business environment to boost more private investment, and equally by investing more in the training of young people.

For China to continue to achieve great things in Africa and sustain the flourishing relationship it enjoys with the region, Beijing needs to put youth at the heart of all its cooperation. The government needs to encourage them by pushing Chinese firms to engage more young Africans when they undertake their investments in the region and also to relax some of its employment rules in China to allow more fresh African graduates to have opportunities to be a part of the work-force in the country.

References

1) "Africa: Study Reveals Chinese Companies Pay & Train Workers to Similar Standards as Non-Chinese Companies." Business & Human Rights Resource Centre, 17 July 2019, www.business-humanrights.org/en/africa-study-reveals-chinese-companies-pay-train-workers-to-similar-standards-as-non-chinese-companies.

2) "Africa's Jobless Youth Cast a Shadow over Economic Growth | Africa Renewal." United Nations, United Nations, www.un.org/africarenewal/magazine/special-edition-youth-2017/africas-jobless-youth-cast-shadow-over-economic-growth.

3) "Africa's Jobless Youth Cast a Shadow over Economic Growth | Africa Renewal." United Nations, United Nations, www.un.org/africarenewal/magazine/special-edition-youth-2017/africas-jobless-youth-cast-shadow-over-economic-growth.

4) Connecting the Dreams of Youth, Writing a New Chapter of China-Africa Friendship: 3rd China-Africa Youth Festival Opens in Beijing, focacsummit.mfa.gov.cn/eng/pthd_1/t1578636.htm.

5) "China-Africa Ties Should Create Jobs for the Youth." Www.sidint.net, www.sidint.net/content/china-africa-ties-should-create-jobs-youth.

6) "Emerging Adulthood." Noba, nobaproject.com/modules/emerging-adulthood.

7) "Facing the Growing Unemployment Challenges in Africa." Facing the Growing Unemployment Challenges in Africa, 20 Jan. 2016, www.ilo.org/africa/media-centre/pr/WCMS_444474/lang--en/index.htm.

8) "Youth Employment in Africa (Africa)." Youth Employment in Africa (Africa), www.ilo.org/africa/areas-of-work/youth-employment/lang--en/index.htm.

9) "Youth Employment in Sub-Saharan Africa." World Bank, www.worldbank.org/en/programs/africa-regional-studies/publication/youth-employment-in-sub-saharan-africa.

10) Adams AV, Johansson de Silva S, Razmara S. Improving skills development in the informal sector: strategies for sub-Saharan Africa. Washington, DC: World Bank; 2013.

11) Betcherman, Gordon, and Themrise Khan. "Jobs for Africa's Expanding Youth Cohort: a Stocktaking of Employment Prospects and Policy Interventions." SpringerLink, Springer Berlin Heidelberg, 12 July 2018, link.springer.com/article/10.1186/s40176-018-0121-y.

12) Betcherman, Gordon, and Themrise Khan. "Jobs for Africa's Expanding Youth Cohort: a Stocktaking of Employment Prospects and Policy Interventions." SpringerLink, Springer Berlin Heidelberg, 12 July 2018, link.springer.com/article/10.1186/s40176-018-0121-y.

13) Boosting youth employment in Africa: what works and why? Report of the conference hosted by INCLUDE and the Ministry of Foreign Affairs 30 May 2017

14) Cleland, J. (2017). Population growth, employment, and livelihoods: the triple challenge. Journal of Demographic Economics, 83(01), 51–61

15) Développement, Agence Française de, and Objectif-Developpement. "Supporting Youth Insertion into the African Labor Market." Issuu, issuu.com/objectif-developpement/docs/youth_insertion_web

16) idrc.ca/sites/default/files/sp/Documents%20EN/Youth_Employment_Sub-Saharan_Africa_WEB_FINAL.pdf

17) Tilman Altenburg Head, Transformation of Economic and Social Systems Programme, German Development Institute / Deutsches Institut für Entwicklungspolitik (DIE)

18) 胡雨濛 . "JOBS FOR AFRICA." JOBS FOR AFRICA - World - Chinadaily.com.cn, www.chinadaily.com.cn/a/201803/31/WS5abe80aba3105cdcf6515763.html.

YOUR KNOWLEDGE HAS VALUE

- We will publish your bachelor's and master's thesis, essays and papers

- Your own eBook and book - sold worldwide in all relevant shops

- Earn money with each sale

Upload your text at www.GRIN.com and publish for free